THE

CREATIVE

POWER

OF

YOUR

WORDS

by GiGi Allen

The Creative Power of Your Words
ISBN-13: 978-1-49217-323-6
Copyright © 2011 by GiGi Allen

Glory to God Publications
P.O. Box 5425
San Mateo, CA 94402
www.victoryic.org

Dedication

To my loving parents
Ron and Kay

Contents

Chapter 1

The Power of Your Words in the Family

The heart of the wise teacheth his mouth.
—Proverbs 16:23

Words Affect Your Future

Many years ago, I had a tremendous opportunity to observe the powerful impact words make on a person's life.

One evening, I was invited to an older gentleman's home while he was babysitting two of his grandchildren. The two boys were brothers, close in age. They had just been put to bed, so we walked to their room to say "goodnight." I noticed both boys had cassette players and headsets on their beds. But while the older boy had the headset on and was listening, the younger boy kept the equipment near his head, refusing to listen.

The grandfather told me both boys were getting poor grades, Ds in fact, and both were playing Little League baseball. Although they both wanted to excel, neither of them were doing well. The grandfather wanted to help the boys, so he invested in teaching tapes created to build children up, specifically in the areas of grades and sports. The words on the tapes were positive, with encouraging comments such as, "You are a success," "you are smart," or "you can get good grades."

The grandfather asked the younger boy to listen to the tapes, but the boy snapped, "I don't want to! It hurts my ears." With an attitude, he pushed the cassette player away from his head, while the older boy laid there soaking up the words on the tapes.

For several months, the older boy continued to listen to the encouraging cassettes.

A few years later, I received a report back on those two boys. The younger boy continued with poor grades, dropped out of baseball, and eventually dropped out of high school. Last I heard of him, he was in a halfway house and was giving his mother much heartache.

The older boy, by contrast, who had continued to listen to the words on the tapes, changed his grades from Ds to straight As, and—as a result—was put on the Honor Roll. He received a baseball scholarship to a college and continued on the Dean's List.

Listening to words on a tape at night before falling asleep was such a simple little thing. And yet, it had such a tremendous impact on the life of the one that was willing to do it. It literally changed the direction of his life. The positive words he heard—words full of life—helped him succeed. This grandfather had wisdom, didn't he?—He knew the powerful impact words can make on a person's life. **The words we listen to affect us. The words we speak affect us.**

Proverbs teaches us about the power of our words.

Proverbs 15:4
A wholesome tongue is a tree of life...

Proverbs 12:18
There is that speaketh like the piercings of a sword: but the tongue of the wise is health.

Those Scriptures show us that

- We can be intentional with our words and make them work for us.

- We can speak positive words over our children, our family members, our co-workers, and ourselves.

- We can be a blessing to those around us by speaking words that encourage.

- Wise people are careful with their words.

Speak Words That Change Your Thinking

A friend of mine in college had a stepfather who had called her stupid for many years while growing up. Although she was a beautiful, intelligent woman, who was able to get into college, she was still convinced that she was stupid. Hearing that word over and over had caused it to take root. Even though it was false, it had damaged her self-image.

She brought this issue up often, so I knew it bothered her. I tried to tell her it was not true, but because she had heard it so many times, it was going to take some work to change her thinking. So I encouraged her to pull Scriptures out of the Bible that addressed her situation, such as

1 Corinthians 2:16
...We have the mind of Christ.

1 Corinthians 1:30
But of him are ye in Christ Jesus, who of God is made unto us wisdom...

I counseled her to speak those Scriptures over herself, especially when the old thought of being referred to as stupid came back to her. After doing this for some time, she called me one day and said, "Guess what? It worked. I no longer think of myself as stupid."

The Word of God is wonderful. It cut through the wrong words that had been spoken and through the lie she had believed. She spoke words of life and truth over herself, such as John 8:32, "And ye shall know the truth, and the truth shall make you free."

She was wise to apply Proverbs 16:23 that says, "The heart of the wise teacheth his mouth." She applied and spoke the Word of God which changed her thinking and her self-image.

Words Affect Your Child's Development

How do our words affect our children?

It is common for them to parrot back what they hear. If kind words are used with them, they will use kind words with others. If they are in a household where swearing and name-calling is allowed, that is what comes out of their mouths outside of the home. Children grow spiritually and emotionally by the words they hear. They need to hear positive, faith-filled words that build them up. It is so much better to tell a child, "You can do it," "use your patience," or "keep trying," than it is to say, "Move out of the way, you are too slow," "you can't do it," or "I will have to do it for you." One builds up and is in line with Philippians 4:13, which says, "I can do all things through Christ which strengtheneth me," while the other tears down.

Children are like little sponges. They soak up and believe what they are told. If you tell them they can do anything, they will believe it. If you tell them with God all things are possible, they will believe it. If you tell them they are intelligent, kind, athletic, strong, brave, loving, and patient, they will rise up to those words. **Words of love and life cause people to rise to their full potential.**

I was blessed to have been raised in a home full of love created by encouraging parents. But I have visited homes where bitter and critical words produced an atmosphere cold as ice.

We often spend a lot of time choosing the right colors, the right furniture, and the right decorations to create a cozy ambiance. But our words—though invisible—contribute much to the atmosphere in our homes.

Words can make a home comfortable or uncomfortable!

Words and Marriage

Ephesians 4:29
Let no corrupt communication proceed out of your mouth, but that which is good to the use of edifying that it may minister grace unto the hearers.

My husband and I once counseled a couple who had problems in their marriage.

When I asked the husband, "How often do you tell your wife that you love her?," she responded before he could answer and said: "Never!"

Finally, he replied, "I don't have to *tell* her, she *knows* it already. I married her, didn't I?"

—Ouch!

We explained that it's important to express love with deeds *and* with words. **Love needs to be communicated!** A love atmosphere is created with love words.

I have noticed that the more my husband and I say to each other, "I love you," the more our love grows. Those words not only express love, but they also communicate strength, security, commitment, and faithfulness. Speaking those words puts love in the air.

When you buy a plant and bring it home, how many times do you water it? Once and then quit?— No! The plant would die. Likewise, marriages and relationships need to be nurtured continuously with words of love.

Couples that threaten their partners with divorce run the risk of ending up in divorce. Why? —Because that is what they have been saying! They have created an atmosphere of divorce.

Love is patient. Love is kind. In a marriage, we obviously become familiar and comfortable with each other. And yet, we need to remember to be careful with our words. We want to choose words that demonstrate love, patience and kindness—words that feed the love in our relationships. Words are like seeds. If we sow love, kindness, and encouragement today, we will reap love, kindness, and encouragement in the future.

Have you been speaking blessings over your family relationships? If you have, wonderful! But if you haven't, the good news is that you can start saying positive words in your home today and begin to create the kind of atmosphere you desire.

Chapter 2

Your Words Shape Your Life

For verily I say unto you, That whosoever
shall say unto this mountain, Be thou removed,
and be thou cast into the sea; and shall not doubt
in his heart, but shall believe that those things
which he saith shall come to pass; he shall have
whatsoever he saith.
—Mark 11:23

You Must Have What You Say!

Let's take a closer look at the way words work to affect your life.

Jesus said, "He shall **have** whatsoever he **saith**." Notice that Jesus used the word "saith" or "says" three times, while He used the word "believe" only once, which shows that He emphasized *saying*! In this case Jesus didn't say a person shall have whatsoever he *believes*. He said a person shall have whatsoever he ***says***![1]

9

Now look at the word "shall" in this verse.

Jesus said, "Those things which he saith 'shall' come to pass; he 'shall' have whatsoever he saith." The original Greek word translated "shall" is the strongest declarative word possible. The word "shall" also means "must." So the verse could read, "those things which he saith **must** come to pass; **he must have whatsoever he saith.**" He *must* have the words he speaks!

A few years ago, I borrowed some books and videos from our local library. When the time came to return them, I could not find one of the video covers, so I began walking around the house saying, "Has anyone seen the cover to the video? I can't find it." My seven-year-old son said, "Mom, you are saying the wrong thing. You should say, "I *can* find the video cover."

He was right! I had taught him Mark 11:23, and he was applying it. Quickly, I changed my words; instead of saying that I could not find the video cover, I began to say, "I *can* find it!" A little later my son and I were playing, wrestling on my bedroom floor. I turned my head, and there was the video cover under the bed. Without even looking for it, I found it.

I had been looking for the missing video cover all over the house without success, but after changing my words to speak the desired result instead of the problem, I found it.

After sharing this story in a class, one man applied it to his car keys. Later, he told me that—in the past—every time he had misplaced his keys, he said, "I can't find my keys." He often spent a long time looking for them. But when he misplaced his keys again, he said, "I *can* find my keys," and he found them right away. He applied this principle several times, and each time he found his keys much faster than before, he realized, "This actually works!"

You see, **it's more effective to speak the desired result than to continue to speak the problem!**

Create Your World With Your Words

The principle of speaking the desired result can be applied to bigger areas in life.

A friend of mine wanted to get married. Although he had been dating, he had not found anyone that he wanted to marry, so he decided to take Mark 11:23 seriously and wrote out a list of ten qualities he wanted his future wife to have.

He taped the list of desired qualities to his bathroom mirror and for six months, every morning while shaving, he spoke those qualities out loud over his future wife.

After some time, someone set up a blind date for him. He drove to the other side of Oklahoma to meet the young woman. On his way home, he realized that she loved the Lord, that she was a singer, and that she was beautiful. She had even won the Miss Tulsa Beauty Pageant. In fact, she had all of the ten qualities on his list. They married a year later. He received what he had said.

When I was just finishing college, my roommate Betsy and I were sitting in our living room one night, and—just for fun—I decided to make up a guy for a date. I decided that he was tall with dark hair. He was working in the real estate business, he drove a red convertible, and his name was Brad. I had always liked that name. We laughed.

My roommate suggested, "Well, he needs a last name." I agreed. So she picked up a magazine from our coffee table and started thumbing through it, looking for last names. She came across an "Ethan Allen" furniture ad and said, "Here is one! How about 'Allen'?" I replied, "Yeah, that's pretty good, but let's go through the magazine to see if we don't find anything better." We tried different last names to go with "Brad," but when we didn't find anything better, we decided his last name would be "Allen." "Brad Allen." We giggled.

A few weeks later, my roommate and I went out, and met two young men. We talked about church. It was exciting to find good-looking men in California that went to church and talked about God. One of them, Brad, knew my former roommate and had even been childhood friends with her boyfriend. We knew a few people in common, and yet we had never met or even heard of each other.

One night a month later, the phone rang, it was Brad. He said he got my phone number from a mutual friend. After chatting for a little while, I found out that he was a real estate appraiser, and his last name was Allen—Brad Allen!

Betsy and I were shocked. Three years later, Brad and I were married.

That night in our living room, Betsy and I were just playing. We were playing with words. Words are powerful, even when you are playing!

God Told Moses to Speak to the Rock

The creative power of our words is not only a New Testament principle. In the Book of Numbers, the Bible shows us that circumstances will line up with our words.

Numbers 20:7-8
And the Lord spake unto Moses saying,
Take the rod, and gather thou the assembly together,
thou, and Aaron thy brother, and speak ye unto the rock
before their eyes; and it shall give forth his water and
thou shalt bring forth to them water out of the rock: so
thou shalt give the congregation and their beasts drink.

After the exodus from Egypt, when the Israelites were wandering in the wilderness on the way to the Promised Land, they complained that there was no water. So God instructed Moses to assemble them. He told Moses to speak to a rock in front of their eyes in order to bring drinking water out of it. But instead of *speaking* to the rock, Moses *struck* the rock twice with his rod. Because of his disobedience, he could not enter the Promised Land.

Was God being unfair?—Never! Why was it so important that Moses *spoke* to the rock?

Some say the significance was that the rock was a type of Christ (1 Corinthians 10:4). But it seems that this event was also a foretelling of Mark 11:23, in which Jesus declares that, "Those things which he saith shall come to pass." God wanted it **said** in front of all of the people. Isn't that interesting?

God said to Moses "**you**" shall bring forth water. He did not say, "I will." He said, "*You will.*" Moses was supposed to tell the rock what to do, and it would have obeyed him. How do we know that? Because God had told Moses the intended outcome, even before Moses did anything. God said that the rock would bring forth water when Moses spoke to it. So Moses didn't have to hit the rock. All he had to do was speak to it. Why?—Because God said so!

Had Moses obeyed God, and spoken to the rock instead of striking it, this story would have been a perfect demonstration of speaking to a mountain and causing it to obey. Before the eyes of the entire assembly of the Israelites, it would have shown the creative power of the spoken word. It would have shown that we will have what we say.

Chapter 3

The Creative Power of Words

In the beginning God created
the Heaven and the earth.
And the earth was without form, and void;
and darkness was upon the face of the deep. And the Spirit
of God moved upon the face of the waters.
And God said, Let there be light:
and there was light.
And God saw the light, that it was good:
and God divided the light from the darkness.
—Genesis 1:1-4

Through faith we understand that the worlds were framed
by the Word of God, so that things which are seen were not
made of things which do appear.
—Hebrews 11:3

God Created the World with Words

Jesus Himself used the creative power of His
Words to affect circumstances. We have records of Him

rebuking a storm, causing a fig tree to wither, and raising Lazarus from the dead—all with His Words.

Let's examine those verses again about the creation of the world. How do they say God created the world?

—He used His **Words** to **speak** it into being!

The New American Standard Bible says in Hebrews 11:3, "The worlds were prepared by the word of God." So something visible was created from something invisible—from **words**!

Spoken words are not visible. And yet, words are all around us, even though we cannot see them. Simply turn on a radio, and you can pick them up.

One time, when I was teaching a Bible School class on this subject, I used the following illustration:

I wrote words on a long piece of banner paper. Then I folded the paper very small and taped it to the bottom of a lid of a glass jar so that it was not visible. I held what seemed to be an empty glass jar up in front of the class.

"What do you see?" I asked.

"Nothing," the students replied.

"What is in the jar?" I asked again.

"Air," one student responded.

"Yes, air. But is there anything else in it?" I asked a third time.

"No," the students replied.

"Are you sure?" I said finally.

I opened the lid and unfolded the long piece of paper with words all over it.

Just because they could not see the words did not mean that the words were not there!

Genesis 1:1-4 tells us God created the world with His Words. The Spirit of God—or we could say the power of God—was moving upon the face of the waters. **Although God's power was present, nothing happened until God** *spoke.* So how was the world created?—By God's spoken, faith-filled Words!

Speaking in Line with God's Word

We were created in the image of God. God created us as speaking beings, equipped with a similar creative ability. So our own faith-filled words activate the power of God on our behalf.

The power of the Holy Spirit was present on the earth before God spoke, and the same Holy Spirit power is present within us, because He lives inside every born-again believer. And yet, like in creation, nothing happens until we *activate* His power. How are we supposed to do that?—By *speaking*! By believing and speaking, to be specific.

So what are we supposed to say?

Jeremiah 1:12 NASB says, "Then the LORD said to me, … 'I am watching over My word to perform it.'" Notice that it is **His Word that He will act on.** So He is telling us that, **when we speak in line with His Word, He will perform it in our lives. When we consistently speak forth God's promises, they are created and brought into manifestation in our lives.**

The angels also help perform God's Word. In Psalm 103:20 NASB, the Bible says, "Bless the LORD, you His angels. Mighty in strength, who perform His word. Obeying the voice of His word!" The Bible says the angels are **"Obeying the voice of His word." So speaking the promises of God over your life gives the angels something to perform on your behalf.**

Several years ago, while I was in Florida, I wanted to visit my brother. I was told that it was a three-hour drive to his house. Since this was supposed to be a short visit, I planned to drive there and back in one day. But the drive turned out much longer than three hours. On my way back home, on a remote stretch of highway with very few exits and without any big cities to spend the night in, the sun went down, and I started to get tired. For a moment I considered pulling off to the side of the highway, which was not a good option, but neither was driving tired.

Suddenly I thought to myself, "Wait a minute. I have the Holy Spirit on the inside of me! He never gets tired! So I began to paraphrase Scripture and speak it over myself out loud. I said things like, "I have the power of the Holy Spirit that raised Jesus Christ from the dead on the inside of me, and that power is quickening my mortal body," (based on Romans 8:11), "I am strong in the Lord and the strength of His might," (based on Ephesians 6:10), and "In Him I live and move and have my being," (based on Acts 17:28). I repeated these words several times and I added my own faith-filled words, such as, "I'm alert, I'm quick, and I'm wide awake!"

Within a few seconds, my entire body was energized. I physically felt more awake. Of course, had I continued to feel tired, I would have pulled over. But God energized my body. The power of God is better than coffee! I found a wonderful Christian radio station and sang the rest of the way home, full of joy and energy as though it was mid day.

So what had happened on that drive home?—By speaking faith-filled words, I drew on the power of God! I knew that Mark 11:23 says that we shall have whatsoever we say. So instead of speaking out what my body felt, I spoke out the desired result based on the Word of God, then God took hold with me and brought it to pass. He is faithful. He watches over His Word to perform it.

The God-Kind-of-Faith

We are told to walk by faith not by sight. We are to walk by faith in God and His Word not by the sense realm, that which we can see and feel. Walking by faith pleases God.

But, how does the Bible define faith?

Let's look at the definition from the Book of Hebrews.

Hebrews 11:1 AMP
NOW FAITH is the assurance (the confirmation, the title deed) of the things [we] hope for, being the proof of things [we] do not see *and* the conviction of their reality [faith perceiving as real fact what is not revealed to the senses].

According to Scripture, faith is defined as the evidence of something unseen—of something that is "not revealed to the senses."

Genesis 1:3 says, "And God said, Let there be light: and there was light." Verse four says, "And God saw the light, that it was good...."

Notice the order of the events. God *first* spoke it, and *then* He saw it!

In verse three, God spoke light into being, and then, in verse four, He saw it. In the beginning, the Holy Spirit had already been over the face of the earth, but nothing happened until God spoke! This shows us how God used faith when He created the world: the "God-kind-of-faith" says it before it can be seen! Romans 4:17 NASB says that God is a God who "calls into being that which does not exist."

This works for us too. Speaking faith-filled words based on the Word of God activates the power of the Holy Spirit and brings our words into manifestation in the natural realm.

Let's look at Mark 11:22-24.

Mark 11:22-24

And Jesus answering saith unto them, Have faith in God.

For verily I say unto you, That whosoever shall say unto this mountain, Be thou removed, and be thou cast into the sea; and shall not doubt in his heart, but shall believe that those things which he saith shall come to pass; he shall have whatsoever he saith.

Therefore I say unto you, What things soever ye desire, when ye pray, believe that ye receive them, and ye shall have them.

The margin of the King James Bible reads that Jesus' statement, "Have faith in God," actually translates from the Greek as "**Have the God-kind-of-faith**." What does this Scripture tell us the "God-kind-of-faith" does? It believes that those things which are spoken happen.

This Spiritual Law Works for Anyone

Who is qualified to speak and see his words come to pass? The Bible says "**whosoever**" qualifies! "Whosoever" is anyone. That means we all qualify. Why? Because Jesus said so!

Does this Scripture only apply to Christians?

No! We can see it fulfilled in people's lives, whether or not they believe in God. This Scripture is a spiritual law, just as gravity is a natural law. Gravity is a force that operates whether or not someone believes in it. When someone drops a ball, the ball falls to the ground, whether or not he believes in gravity. In a similar way, the spiritual law that "he shall have whatsoever he says" is in operation, whether or not someone realizes it.

I once heard an interview with a successful actor who was talking about his childhood. He said he had grown up in the ghetto of New York City, raised by a single mom. Life had been hard. They had lived on welfare. However he said his mother had always told him that he could do *anything* when he grew up. She had told him that some day he would get out of the ghetto and be successful. The words she had spoken had created faith and confidence in him. He attributed his success to his mother, whose positive words gave him hope and vision. Her words were fulfilled: he did get out of the ghetto, and he did become a successful actor.

Faith-filled words can change circumstances!

"Faith is released by speaking.
If you are silent, you lose by default". [2]
—Mark Hankins

Chapter 4

Consider Your Words

Let the words of my mouth, and the meditation
of my heart, be acceptable in thy sight, O LORD,
my strength, and my redeemer.
—Psalm 19:14

Let no corrupt communication proceed out of your mouth,
but that which is good to the use of edifying,
that it may minister grace unto the hearers.
—Ephesians 4:29

Let no foul *or* polluting language *nor*
evil word *nor* unwholesome *or* worthless talk [ever]
come out of your mouth, but only such [speech]
as is good and beneficial to the spiritual progress of others,
as is fitting to the need *and* the occasion,
that it may be a blessing *and* give grace (God's favor)
to those who hear it.
And do not grieve the Holy Spirit of God
[do not offend or vex or sadden Him]....
—Ephesians 4:29, 30 AMP

God wants us to speak faith-filled words. He wants our words to create an atmosphere of faith that blesses us and those who hear us.

In Ephesians 4:29 the Amplified Bible teaches that there are two main categories of words: those we are not supposed to use, and those we are supposed to use. Let's begin with the first category. It says "**let no foul** *or* **polluting language . . . [ever] come out of your mouth.**" So what kinds of words are we not supposed to use?—Foul language! When is it acceptable to use foul language? If someone provokes you in anger? Or perhaps if you hit your thumb with a hammer during a home improvement project?—No! The Bible says to let no foul language "**ever**" come out of your mouth. "Ever" is a key word here. Foul language should *never* be used!

Words of Unbelief Can Cost You

In Ephesians 4:29 AMP, the Bible says to let no "**evil word**" come out of your mouth.

What do you think is an "evil word?"

When the Israelites had reached the borders of the Promised Land, God told Moses to send a man from each tribe into the land—a land God had said He would give to them, a land filled with milk and honey, a **Promised Land**!

Now read their report.

Numbers 13:30-32
And Caleb stilled the people before Moses, and said, Let

24

us go up at once, and possess it; for we are well able to overcome it.
But the men that went up with him said, We be not able to go up against the people; for they are stronger than we. And they brought up an EVIL report of the land which they had searched unto the children of Israel, saying, The land, through which we have gone to search it, is a land that eateth up the inhabitants thereof; and all the people that we saw in it are men of a great stature.

Notice that verse 32 says, "And they brought up an **evil report**." Why was their report evil?—It was evil because it was a report of doubt and unbelief! They did not believe the Word of God, which means that their report directly opposed the Word of God.

So according to Scripture, we see that **evil words are words of unbelief that contradict God's Word.** We have been talking about the blessing of speaking faith-filled words. Likewise, Hebrews 11:6 says, "Without faith it is impossible to please Him," and Ephesians 4:30 NASB says, "Do not grieve the Holy Spirit of God . . ." which means do not offend or sadden Him. If we want God's blessing, we should say the same thing He says, and not contradict Him with words.

Accountable for All We Say

The Scripture says, "Let no... **worthless** talk [ever] come out of your mouth."

What are "worthless" words?—They are idle, futile, or useless words. They are simply words that don't do anything at all!—Unproductive words!

Let's look at what Jesus says in the following verses.

Matthew 12:35-37
A good man out of the good treasure of the heart bringeth forth good things: and an evil man out of the evil treasure bringeth forth evil things.
But I say unto you, That every idle word that men shall speak, they shall give account thereof in the day of judgment. For by thy words thou shalt be justified, and by thy words thou shalt be condemned.

He says that men will have to give an account for **every idle word** they speak.

Have you ever been around someone who talks and talks and talks, but never really says anything? Often those individuals get off track and can't even remember what they were saying anyway. If they don't value their words, how is the listener supposed to appreciate them? You can learn a lot about people by the words they speak. Jesus says in verse 35 that good words come out of a good heart.

Speaking Words of Life

Now consider the second category in Ephesians 4:29, the words that we *are* supposed to speak. I have the pleasure of working with an assistant who has trained his mouth to be—as the Proverb says—a "fountain of life." He is always encouraging others with his faith-filled words. It's a joy and a privilege to work with a person like that! People seem to gravitate to him for prayer and encouragement.

Ephesians 4:29 KJV says to use communication "which is good to the use of edifying, that it may minister grace unto the hearers." This tells us that our speech should be beneficial for the spiritual progress of others.

Proverbs 10:11 NASB
The mouth of the righteous is a fountain of life,…

Proverbs 18:4 NASB
The words of a man's mouth are deep waters;
The fountain of wisdom is a bubbling brook.

Colossians 4:6
Let your speech be always with grace, seasoned with salt, that ye may know how ye ought to answer every man.

You see, our words are supposed to work for ourselves and for others!

As I look back over my life, I have realized that the friends I have chosen have always been sensitive, considerate, and careful with their words. Wouldn't you rather have people around you who support you with positive words, than those who discourage you with their negativity?

In Exodus 17:8-13, when the Israelites fought the Amalekites on their way to the Promised Land, they prevailed only as long as Moses' hand was held up. Once it dropped, the Amalekites began to win the battle. So when Moses' hand became heavy, Aaron and Hur supported it, keeping it steady all day, and the Israelites won the war. I would imagine that when Aaron and Hur were holding up Moses arm physically, they were also contributing spiritually. Had they been saying, "We're never going to win; it's hopeless," even though they were helping physically, it's unlikely that Moses would have allowed them to stay.

There are battles in all of our lives. It's good to surround yourself with people who can speak the right words in the right circumstances. It's also good to be that person for others.

My assistant befriended a young woman who works at our local bank. He had been speaking loving, faith-filled words to her ever since they had met. One day, she opened up and shared how her husband recently and unexpectedly passed away. She told my assistant how much she had needed his kind words, which were spoken even before he knew about her situation. A total stranger who was hurting confided in him because of the encouraging words he had spoken to her.

There are opportunities around us every day. As we stay sensitive to the Holy Spirit, we can use our words to be a tree of life to those around us. We may not know what people are going through, but the Holy Spirit does. As we train our mouths to be a source of life, God can use us to speak positive, uplifting words even in adverse circumstances.

The Wisdom of Being Slow to Speak

There are situations that can make saying the right words at the right time challenging. The Bible says that the wise control their lips, while fools often speak fast and without thinking. Many words without thought lead to sin and can be damaging to ourselves and to others. Let's see what the Bible says about being careful with your words, even in situations that could provoke you to respond negatively.

James 1:19
Wherefore, my beloved brethren, let every man be swift to hear, slow to speak, slow to wrath.

Proverbs 10:19–20 NASB
When there are many words, transgression is unavoidable, But he who restrains his lips is wise. The tongue of the righteous is *as* choice silver,

Proverbs 13:3
He that keepeth his mouth keepeth his life: But he that openeth wide his lips shall have destruction.

Proverbs 15:28
The heart of the righteous studieth to answer: But the mouth of the wicked poureth out evil thing.

How did Jesus respond when the Pharisees tried to corner Him with His Words? In John chapter eight, the Pharisees brought Him a woman who had been caught in adultery. The Old Testament law said specifically that she should be stoned for her sin, but now Jesus was bringing a new and better covenant based on love and forgiveness. The Pharisees thought they had Him trapped when they asked in anger and in religious righteousness what should be done with her. But Jesus remained silent. He bent down and drew in the sand. There has been much speculation about what He drew. Some have guessed that He wrote out the sins of those that were accusing her. We don't know for sure.

What we do know is that **He did not respond immediately.**

Instead, He took His time before He answered, possibly to pray. Remember in this same chapter, in verse 28, He says, "I do nothing of myself; but as my Father hath taught me, I speak these things." What is clear is that He did not respond until He had the wisdom to do so. Then He said brilliantly, "Let him that is without sin cast the first stone." The Pharisees could not trap Him because He had the wisdom to restrain His words.

The Wisdom of Remaining Silent

In the Proverbs, you can see that sometimes it's best not to say anything at all.

Proverbs 17:27-28
He that hath knowledge spareth his words:
and a man of understanding is of an excellent spirit.
Even a fool, when he holdeth his peace, is counted wise:
and he that shutteth his lips is esteemed a man of understanding.

I remember one instance when a woman was slandering my husband and me, right after we had helped her in a situation. Although mean and hurtful comments were directed at us, I kept my mouth shut. I did not say anything in our defense. Instead I held my tongue and prayed silently. Then I reached out my arms and hugged her. At first it felt like what I would imagine hugging a porcupine would feel like. But soon she softened in my arms. I was able to love her even though she had been directly and intentionally hurtful.

My mom used to say when I was growing up, and maybe you've heard it, "If you don't have anything nice to say, then don't say anything at all."

There is wisdom in waiting and praying before responding! And there is wisdom in being silent.

Keeping Your Word

Being careful with our words also means to keep our word.

In Matthew 5:37 and James 5:12, the Bible tells us to let our "yes" be yes and our "no" be no. What does that mean?—It means to be a person of your word! If you say you're going to do something, follow through and do it. If you make a commitment, keep it. If you say you're going to be somewhere at a specific time, then be there at that time.

Now let's see what the Bible says about the Words of Jesus.

John 1:1
In the beginning was the Word, and the Word was with God, and the Word was God.

Jesus was and is so true to His Word that He can be called "The Word." We are supposed to be His imitators, and therefore we are to honor our word.

Why is this so important?

My grandfather, a man of his word, is a good example. If he said he would do something, he would do it. One time he said he would help me build a closet. He said, "I'll be at your place at x time." That morning I looked out of the window and saw him parked in front of my house, just sitting in his car. He sat there for about ten minutes. When he finally came to the door I said, "Grandpa what were you doing? I saw you out in front. Why didn't you come in?" "He responded, "Well, I told you I'd be here at x time, and it wasn't x time yet." He could be counted on, and people around him knew that.

When you keep your word, you have more faith and confidence in the words you speak.

When Jesus said He was the resurrection and the life, even before He had gone to the cross, He could be trusted. He followed through on His Word. Aren't you glad He kept His Word? The Word of God can be trusted, which is why we can count on all of God's promises.

Since we are being conformed to the image of Christ, we need to keep our word, just as He keeps His Word. People know us by our words.

Chapter 5

Confession is the Stepping Stone to Possession

For by thy words thou shalt be justified,
and by thy Words thou shalt be condemned.
—Matthew 12:37

That if thou shalt confess with thy mouth
the Lord Jesus, and shalt believe in thine heart
that God hath raised him from the dead,
thou shalt be saved.
For with the heart man believeth unto
righteousness; and with the mouth confession
is made unto salvation.
—Romans 10:9, 10

What Does "Confession" Mean?

Our words affect our circumstances and the
atmosphere that surrounds us. With our words we have

created the life we are living. Our words not only affect our life here on earth but also where we will spend eternity!

In the Book of Romans, the Bible says, "With the mouth confession is made unto salvation." According to this Scripture, salvation comes through "confession."

But what does "confession" mean?

Confession simply means to agree with God.

Most of us are familiar with "confessing" our sins, but we are also to confess our faith. The Greek word translated into "confession" means "to say the same thing." So there is also a positive side to confession. We are to agree with God and to say the same thing as God.

Most Everything We Receive from God Comes by Confession

Besides salvation, what else comes by "believing God and saying the same thing as God"?—**Everything else**! Everything we receive from God comes by confessing and believing (unless it is a manifestation of the gifts of the Holy Spirit). We believe and "confess" to activate the promises of God in our lives.

Salvation is a good example. Jesus Christ is the Savior of all men. And yet, not all men are saved. Why? Although salvation has been provided for all men, not all men have received it. The promise of salvation has not been activated in the lives of all men, because not all men have believed and "confessed" Jesus Christ as Lord and Savior. It is God's will for everyone to be saved, but God gives everyone the freedom to choose. Salvation is a free gift from God. It does not come by works, so that no one can boast.

We have seen that confession is "made unto" salvation. But confession is also "made unto" such things as freedom, victory, blessings, prosperity, joy, etc. We believe and speak our way into those blessings. **Confession is the stepping stone to possession!**

Let's look at this concept in the Book of Hebrews.

Hebrews 4:14 NASB
Therefore, since we have a great high priest who has passed through the heavens, Jesus the Son of God, let us hold fast our confession.

What does the Bible mean by to "hold fast our confession?"

To "hold fast our confession" means to consistently speak faith-filled words which speak the desired outcome into being. We are not to waver or be inconsistent. Victory lies in consistency.

Don't Be Ensnared by Your Words: Agree with God!

For a moment let's look at the opposite effect—the effect of confessing the wrong kinds of words.

Proverbs 6:2
Thou art snared by the words of thy mouth.

The Bible says that our words justify us or condemn us. We are either set free or taken captive by the words of our mouths.

Some years ago, I heard a fabulous teaching on this subject.

A man approached a minister and told him that he wanted to quit smoking, but he couldn't. He had tried many times without success.

The minister gave him some very interesting counsel. He told the man to focus on the words he spoke. While the man was saying, "I can't quit," his own words were defeating him. It's a spiritual law that we will have what we say. The minister told him to change what he had been saying and never to say, "I can't quit" again. Even if he went out to buy more cigarettes, he was to continually say, "I am free from cigarettes. I *can* quit smoking."

At first that might sound like a contradiction. But in fact it's just a choice to say the same thing the Word of God says, rather than verbalizing our physical circumstances or weaknesses.

The Word of God says in 2 Corinthians 3:17, "Where the Spirit of the Lord is, there is liberty," in John 8:32, "And ye shall know the truth, and the truth shall make you free," and in John 8:36, "If the Son therefore shall make you free, ye shall be free indeed."

The man was a believer, so Christ had already set him free. All he needed to do was to believe it and to say it. Why? Because God has already set us free, and all we need to do is believe and act on this Bible promise! The man had been ensnared by the words of his own mouth. Changing what he had been saying and agreeing with God was his way out of the bondage of smoking. The minister told him to say, "Christ has set me free." Even if he had to say it in between puffs and every time he lit up.

The man returned and reported that, within two weeks, he was completely free from cigarettes. He was able to claim the promise of God by staying consistent with his words.

That teaching set me free, too.

I had been trying to quit drinking coffee without much success, but this story helped me to realize that I was trying to get something that I had already been given. I kept trying to get free from it, instead of realizing that—according to the Word of God—I had already been set free. All I had to do was to say it with the words of my mouth in order to receive the manifestation of the promise. As soon as I changed what I was saying, I was completely free from coffee within two weeks!

I tapped into the scriptural principle of confession. And you can do the same.

Blessed or Cursed by Your Words

You see, your words can prosper you. But they can also cause you to fail.

The words we use when we refer to ourselves can cause us to rise to our full potential in Christ, or to fall short. Our words can cause us to overcome life's battles and position us for success. **We are all that the Word of God says we are. We can do all that the Word of God says we can do.** Our words are either in agreement with God, or in opposition to Him. When we say what the Word of God says, we line up with God and give Him something to perform. The Bible says, "I can do all things through Christ who strengthens me" (Philippians 4:13). When we say we *can* do something, we can, but when we say we *can't*, we thwart our success. Our words carry creative spiritual power and affect the outcome.

> **"A spiritual law that few recognize**
> **is that our confession rules us.**
> **It is what we confess with our lips**
> **that really dominates our inner being."** [3]
> **F.F. Bosworth**

Let's look at Mark 11:12-14 and also at verses 20-23 again.

Mark 11:12-14; 20-23 NASB
On the next day, when they left Bethany, He became hungry.
Seeing at a distance a fig tree in leaf, He went to *see* if perhaps He would find anything on it; and when He came to it, He found nothing but leaves, for it was not the season for figs. He said to it, "May no one ever eat fruit from you again!" And His disciples were listening.
. . .

As they were passing by in the morning, they saw the fig tree withered from the roots *up*.
Being reminded, Peter *said to him, "Rabbi, look, the fig

tree which You cursed has withered."
And Jesus *answered saying to them, "Have faith in God. Truly I say to you, whoever says to this mountain, 'Be taken up and cast into the sea,' and does not doubt in his heart, but believes that what he says is going to happen, it will be *granted* him.

Peter said, "The fig tree which You **cursed** has withered." Notice the words Jesus spoke that caused the fig tree to wither. He did not say, "I curse you fig tree!" Rather He simply spoke **negative words** to the tree.

Speaking negatively to something or to someone is speaking a curse!

I know of a person who cursed a huge tree. After cursing that tree, the next day, there was no visible difference. But within a few years, all of the leaves fell off, and the branches became dry and brittle. Someone said, "The tree is going to have to be removed. It died. We think it may have been hit by lightning." Maybe the tree was hit by lightening, we don't know for sure. Either way, its death was a result of the words that had been spoken to it.

Death and Life Are in The Power of The Tongue

When that same person who spoke to the tree prayed for people and cursed cancer, those cancerous growths disappeared. "**Death and life are in the power of the tongue**" (Proverbs 18:21). This does not just work for Jesus. It also works for us. Just as Jesus cursed the fig tree, we can curse cancer and command sickness to leave. Each one of us has this same power inside of us through the Holy Spirit, who is activated by faith-filled words.

Words release blessings or curses. When I send out e-mails, I like to end them with, "God bless you!" I don't do this to be "religious." I do this because I know the power that is contained within those words. I believe that blessings from God are released when those words are spoken or written.

We can see the power of speaking blessings through many of the patriarchs in the Old Testament, such as Isaac blessing Jacob and Esau in Genesis chapter twenty-seven. Before Isaac died, he had spoken blessings over his children, and the Scriptures show us those blessings came to pass.

What an opportunity fathers have to speak over their children, and what opportunities we all have to bless other people with our words!

Have you ever heard people make comments such as, "I hate my life," "my life stinks," "he is driving me crazy," "that kills me," "it scared me to death," or "oh, I just wanted to die?" Well, sometimes people don't think about what they are saying, and bad habits can develop. Mature Christians who understand the power of their words don't talk like that.

The following Scriptures show us that those comments oppose God.

Jeremiah 29:11 NASB
'For I know the plans that I have for you,' declares the Lord, 'plans for welfare and not for calamity to give you a future and a hope.'

John 10:10
The thief cometh not, but for to steal, and to kill, and to destroy: I am come that they might have life, and that they might have it more abundantly.

2 Timothy 1:7
For God hath not given us the spirit of fear; but of power, and of love, and of a sound mind.

If those comments are in opposition to the Word of God, then they are in opposition to God Himself. The careless comments are curses.

Is it a good idea to oppose God? No! Opposing God opens the door to the devil.

The Bible says in Ephesians 4:27, "Neither give place to the devil," in James 4:7, "Resist the devil and he will flee from you," and in 1 Peter 5:8, "Be sober, be vigilant; because your adversary the devil, as a roaring lion, walketh about, seeking whom he may devour."

Words resist the devil or give him access. Words of fear, doubt, failure, sickness, hardship, and lack open the door to the devil, because they are words that agree with what he does. Whether we realize it or not they give him permission to enter a situation.

When Jesus was tempted by the devil in Matthew chapter four, He quoted the Word of God to resist him. In John chapter eight, Jesus says, "I do nothing of myself; but as my Father hath taught me, I speak these things." He said the same thing as God, and therefore He gave the devil no access.

Can we say that about our own words? Can we say that all of our words are full of faith and truth and in line with the Word of God?—Wonderful results follow when that is the case!

Chapter 6

Words That Overcome

**And they overcame him by the blood of the Lamb,
and by the word of their testimony.
—Revelation 12:11**

God wants us to have victory. He wants us to overcome all adversity. We overcome through the "blood of the Lamb," Jesus Christ, but we also overcome by "the word of our testimony."

**—What we choose to say determines
whether or not we overcome!**

David's Overcoming Words

David demonstrated for us the role words played in his battle with Goliath. For forty days, Goliath, challenged the armies of Israel to choose a man who would fight him. Should the Israelite fighter win, the

Philistines would serve Israel, but should Goliath win, the Israelites would become slaves. It was a high-stakes battle for one person to take on! Goliath was taunting the Israelites, who were greatly afraid. But David, the youngest and smallest of them all, was different. His faith was in His God. With only a sling and a stone, he prevailed over the Philistine giant and killed him.

Even before the fight began, David defeated the giant with his words. Based on God's promises, he declared with the words of his mouth what would happen to Goliath, and his words paved the way for victory. David overcame his enemy not just for himself, but for all of Israel. All of Israel was blessed by his words, his faith, and his actions!

In 1 Samuel chapter 17 NASB David spoke:

- Verse 32. David said to Saul, "Let no man's heart fail on account of him; your servant will go and fight with this Philistine."

- Verse 36. When Saul told David he was but a youth, David replied, "Your servant has killed both the lion and the bear; and this uncircumcised Philistine will be like one of them, since he has taunted the armies of the living God."

- Verse 37. And David said, "The Lord who delivered me from the paw of the lion and from the paw of the bear, He will deliver me from the hand of this Philistine."

- Verse 46. David boldly said to Goliath, "This day the LORD will deliver you up into my hands, and I will strike you down... that all the earth may know that there is a God in Israel," . . .

So what did David do here?

- Goliath may have been big, but David knew his God was bigger.

- David testified with boldness what would happen. He spoke the desired result and received what he said.

- David overcame not by traditional armor, sword, or spear, but by the words of his mouth.

We may not have a Goliath in our lives, but we do have an enemy, the devil, who may try to place obstacles into our path. We can be like David and overcome obstacles with our words!

God's Promises

Like David, we are in covenant with God, so we can overcome obstacles with our words. With faith in God we can boldly declare the desired outcome based on God's promises. He has promised us victory and triumph in Christ.

1 Corinthians 15:57
But thanks be to God, which giveth us the victory through our Lord Jesus Christ.

2 Corinthians 2:14
Now thanks be unto God, which always causeth us to triumph in Christ.

Are you willing to step out in faith and boldly declare victory in every area of your life?

It doesn't happen by thinking about it. It happens by speaking it out loud, and by acting on it! Staying consistent with our words is key!

Joshua's and Caleb's Overcoming Words

Matthew 12:37
For by thy words thou shalt be justified, and by thy words thou shalt be condemned.

2 Corinthians 4:13
We having the same spirit of faith, according as it is written, I believed, and therefore have I spoken; we also believe, and therefore speak.

Our lives today are the result of what we have been believing and saying.

Our relationship with God begins by believing and speaking when we accept Jesus Christ into our lives. When a person confesses Jesus Christ as Lord and Savior, he is transferred from the kingdom of darkness to the kingdom of light. Nothing may be felt physically, but the moment one believes and speaks, the transfer occurs. Based on the belief in his heart and the words of his mouth, God recreates a person's spirit when he confesses Jesus.

Just as our relationship with God began by believing and speaking, it continues by using the same principle. With our words, we can put the power of heaven into action on our behalf. However with our words, we can also open the door to the devil.

In the book of Numbers Joshua and Caleb spoke overcoming words. But the other ten spies and the whole congregation had a negative response.

Numbers 14:2-3
And all the children of Israel murmured against Moses and against Aaron: and the whole congregation said unto them, Would God that we had died in the land of Egypt! or would God we had died in this wilderness! And wherefore hath the LORD brought us unto this land, to fall by the sword, that our wives and our children should be a prey? were it not better for us to return into Egypt?

When they saw that the people who occupied the Promised Land were strong and its cities heavily fortified, they grumbled against Moses and Aaron and said that they were not able to take the land. In fact, they said that they would rather return to the land where they had been **slaves or die** than believe God! Although they had personally witnessed incredible signs and wonders when God saved their firstborn sons, parted the Red Sea, and delivered them from Egyptian slavery, they quickly forgot that God is a God who keeps His promises, even in the face of obstacles.

What was the result of their unbelief? Let's look at God's response to Moses.

Numbers 14:28-30 NASB
"Say to them, 'As I live,' says the LORD, 'just as you have spoken in My hearing, so I will surely do to you; (*The original language is in a permissive sense, meaning so He will surely permit or allow to happen*).
your corpses will fall in this wilderness, even all your numbered men, according to your complete number

from twenty years old and upward, who have grumbled against Me. 30 'Surely you shall not come into the land in which I swore to settle you, except Caleb the son of Jephunneh and Joshua the son of Nun.

In verse thirty, God said, "Surely you shall not come into the land in which I swore to settle you, except **Caleb** the son of Jephunneh and **Joshua** the son of Nun." Why did God say that Joshua and Caleb could enter the Promised Land, while the other spies couldn't? The Bible tells us that it was because Caleb had a "different spirit."

Numbers 14:24 NASB
"But my servant Caleb, because he has had a different spirit and has followed Me fully, I will bring into the land which he entered, and his descendants shall take possession of it."

So what had Caleb said that led God to conclude he had a "different spirit?"

Numbers 13:30 NASB
Then Caleb quieted the people before Moses and said, "We should by all means go up and take possession of it, for we will surely overcome it."

Caleb and Joshua were the only spies who could enter the Promised Land because they were the only ones who had agreed with God, saying that they were able to enter in spite of the giants in the land. Notice that everyone in this account received exactly what he said. Those who said they would rather die in the wilderness, died in the wilderness. Joshua and Caleb who said they could overcome and enter the Promised Land, overcame and entered the Promised Land. **God gave them each**

according to their words. Each one of them created their future with their own words.

Our words affect our destiny. What are you saying about your future? You can put your words to work today!

Chapter 7

Thanksgiving Verses Complaining

He who restrains his words has knowledge, . . .
—**Proverbs 17:27 NASB**

Thou art snared with the words of thy mouth,
thou art taken with the words of thy mouth.
—**Proverbs 6:2**

He who guards his mouth and his tongue,
Guards his soul from troubles.
—**Proverbs 21:23 NASB**

God Doesn't Like Complaining

There is wisdom in restraining our words. It is better to use our words to give thanks than it is to complain. When the Israelites saw the giants in the Promised Land, they grumbled against Moses. If you read chapters eleven and twelve in the Book of Numbers, you will see that they did quite a bit of complaining.

They complained about their circumstances, their food, and their leadership.

The following verses show the consequences of complaining.

Numbers 11:1
And when the people complained, it displeased the LORD: and the LORD heard it; and his anger was kindled; and the fire of the LORD burnt among them, and consumed them that were in the uttermost parts of the camp.

Their complaining kindled God's anger. God dislikes complaining. In 1 Corinthians 10:10-11, we see that this Old Testament account was written to teach us what *not* to do.

1 Corinthians 10:10, 11
Neither murmur ye, as some of them also murmured, and were destroyed of the destroyer.
Now all these things happened unto them for ensamples: and they are written for our admonition [instruction], upon whom the ends of the world are come.

Complaining not only angers God; it opens the door for the devil because it is sin. We see that the Israelites were destroyed by the "destroyer," which is the devil, and not by God. It is much better to respond the way Paul did, who said in Philippians 4:11 that he learned to be content in all circumstances.

Give Thanks

Psalm 92:1
It is a good thing to give thanks unto the LORD.

Thessalonians 5:16–18 NASB
Rejoice always;
pray without ceasing;
in everything give thanks; for this is God's will for you
in Christ Jesus.

God's will for us is to give thanks in everything. Notice the scripture says *in* everything, it does not say *for* everything. We don't thank God when bad things happen, He does not cause bad things to happen, the devil does. However we can still be thankful no matter what type of situation we are in. We can keep an attitude of gratitude despite circumstances because we know God is on our side. He loves us. He is always working to bring about the best for us!

In contrast to the Israelites we can look at the life of Paul and Silas. In Acts chapter sixteen, after ministering the gospel, they were beaten and thrown in prison. Unlike the Israelites, they did not complain. In spite of their circumstances they worshiped and praised God. What was the result of keeping a good attitude and not complaining even in a bad situation? Paul and Silas were delivered and set free! Praising and giving thanks keeps us in the will of God.

Have you ever noticed it's a lot more fun to give to someone who is thankful? It makes you want to give him even more.

When my son was younger, he was invited to a birthday party. In preparation we talked about the Bible principle that says it is better to give than to receive. Then I took him to the toy store, and he picked out a large bright-colored dump truck to give as a gift. He carefully chose a toy he would have been excited to receive. He was very excited to give it in anticipation of his friend's joy.

After the party I asked him, "Did your friend like the truck?"

"I don't know" he responded.

Two days later at school, his friend told him that he had taken the dump truck back to the store and picked out something else.

His friend was not thankful. He did not value the gift or appreciate my son's time and thought that had gone into choosing it. As a result, the next year, my son didn't even want to go to his birthday party.

Thankful people receive more.

Be Thankful and Say So

Psalm 109:30
I will greatly praise the LORD with my mouth; yea, I will praise him among the multitude.

Psalm 100:4 AMP
Enter into His gates with thanksgiving *and* a thank offering and into His courts with praise! Be thankful *and* say so to Him, bless *and* affectionately praise His name!

What do these verses say about *how* to give thanks?—With our words! **So let's be thankful and say so!**

While I was attending Bible School, I was led to give a teacher thirty-five dollars. Although this was a lot of money for me at the time, I was not sure he would appreciate such a small gift. Though slightly embarrassed, I obeyed God.

I meekly approached the teacher after class to hand him the check. I will always remember how he responded. He was genuinely thankful and clearly expressed it with his words. Acting like it was thirty-five *thousand* dollars, he prayed for me to receive a return on what I had sowed. It was a blessing to witness how he honored and valued my small gift.

I have enjoyed supporting his ministry on a more consistent basis because of that experience. That teacher set a great example.

There are times that God tells us to give specific amounts of money to specific individuals or ministries, but there are also times when we can choose whom we give to and how much.

Grateful people receive more. Let's be thankful and **say so**!

Chapter 8

Healing Words

> . . . the tongue of the wise is health.
> —Proverbs 12:18

> My son, attend to my words;
> Incline thine ear unto my sayings.
> Let them not depart from thine eyes;
> Keep them in the midst of thine heart.
> For they are life unto those that find them,
> And health to all their flesh.
> —Proverbs 4:20–22

> Incline your ear and hear the words of the wise,
> And apply your mind to my knowledge;
> For it will be pleasant if you keep them within you,
> That they may be ready on your lips.
> —Proverbs 22:17-18 NASB

Words That Bring Healing

Another area in which words play an important role is healing.

My grandfather used to say, "I don't believe in being sick," and he wasn't. When he was in his eighties, every day he still walked seven flights of stairs for exercise instead of taking the elevator. The principle of confession works for healing too.

The Scripture says, "The tongue of the wise is health," which teaches us that **wise people call their bodies healthy**; they know that they will receive according to their words. Calling your body sick, on the other hand, is speaking in opposition to the Word of God.

1 Peter 2:24 says, "Who his own self bare our sins in his own body on the tree, that we, being dead to sins, should live unto righteousness: by whose stripes ye were healed." By the stripes that Jesus took we were healed. There is provision for healing through Jesus just as salvation is through Him. Jesus healed all that came to Him and He is the same yesterday, today and forever. When He sent the disciples out to preach the gospel He also told them to heal the sick.

God promises us health in His Word. Jesus has taken away sickness in the same way He has taken away sin. You may ask, "Then why are so many Christians sick?" Well, there are several possible reasons. Perhaps they don't know the Word of God, or they have been incorrectly taught. They might also have opened the door to the devil through sin or through the words of their own mouths. It is common to hear people, even Christians, talk about being sick.

I remember Mrs. P. sharing the following testimony with me. She was working for a computer company. It was winter, and some employees were arriving to work sick, coughing and wheezing. Others stayed home for the same reason, so Mrs. P. was surrounded by sickness. She could hear other employees making comments like, "Well, it's winter," "It's the flu season," "It's going around," or "I guess I'm going to get it, too." But Mrs. P. was careful with her words and said, "I'm the picture of health!" She never gave sickness access with her words.

One morning during that same week when she arrived at work, she suddenly didn't feel well, just like her co-workers had been saying. Her throat started to hurt when she swallowed. But still, she remained faithful with her words. She sat in front of her computer and quietly quoted Scripture to herself, such as Matthew 8:17, He "Himself took our infirmities, and bare our sicknesses," and 1 Peter 2:24, "by whose stripes ye were healed." It was a battle, because she did not *feel* healed. But she *knew* the truth of God's Word and His promise to her. She *knew* sickness came from the devil, so she refused to give up and instead stood in faith and confessed the Word of God.

By the end of the work day, all the symptoms of sickness had left her. With her words, she had not allowed sickness to enter her body. Consequently, she remained healthy, while most of her co-workers were out sick for a week or more. Again, everyone in this situation received what they said. Healing also comes by confession—by saying the same thing as God.

The Woman with the Issue of Blood

In the Book of Mark, the Bible tells us of a woman who had an "issue of blood" for twelve years. She had seen physicians, spent all she owned, yet her condition grew worse. When she heard about Jesus, she pushed her way through the crowd and touched His cloak saying, "If I may touch but his clothes, I shall be whole" (Mark 5:28). The Amplified Bible says, "For she kept saying, If I only touch his garments, I shall be restored to health." She touched him, and she was healed. This woman **kept saying** she would be healed, and healing is what she received.

Elisha Raises the Shunammite's Son from the Dead

In the Book of 2 Kings, a Shunammite woman's son was raised from the dead. How did her words impact the outcome?

When the prophet Elisha was in Shunem, a Shunammite woman prepared a room for him in her house, so that, when he passed by, he would have a place to stay. He asked what he could do for her in return. Hearing that she did not have children, he prophesied that she would have a son. That son was indeed born, but—at a young age—the boy died in his mother's arms. The Shunammite woman did not tell anyone what had happened, not even her husband, and instead said that she was going to the man of God and would return later. When her husband asked her why she was going there, she said, "**It shall be well**" (2 Kings 4:23).

Why do you think this woman responded in this way? She must have known the importance of her words, because she never changed what she was saying. When she was asked, "Is it well with the child?" she answered, "**It is well**" (2 Kings 4:26). The Bible does not call her a liar. She chose to believe the promise of God over the circumstances. God had promised her a son through the prophet, and she was not going to let go of that promise, so she spoke out the desired result instead of the problem. Consequently, the boy was raised from the dead. It did turn out well. The woman received the words she spoke.

Faith To Be Healed

Many years ago, when I was a young Christian, I suffered from chronic fatigue syndrome; I was exhausted all the time. I kept asking God to heal me, but nothing changed. In spite of that condition, I went to Bible School. I was determined to go.

I still remember my first day of class. One of my Bible teachers, Kenneth E. Hagin, taught from Mark chapter five. He taught about "the woman with the issue of blood," to whom Jesus said, "**Daughter, thy faith hath made thee whole**," and he also read God's definition of faith in the Book of Hebrews. In that class, I realized didn't know God's definition of faith. I thought that faith was believing God could heal me (in the future). But according to the Word of God, that's not faith. That's hope. Why? Because it's future tense! Look at what Paul said in Hebrews 11:1.

Hebrews 11:1 AMP
NOW FAITH is the assurance (the confirmation, the title deed) of the things [we] hope for, being the proof of

things [we] do not see *and* the conviction of their reality [faith perceiving as real fact what is not revealed to the senses].

Faith is now! Faith is to believe that something is done now, and not that it will be done in the future.

Mark 11:24 NASB says, **"Therefore I say to you, all things for which you pray and ask, believe that you have received them, and they will be *granted* you."** Notice that this Scripture says **"you have received."** This means that something is granted when you believe you have received it, which is often before it visibly manifests.

With new understanding, I got out of hope and into faith. I changed what I had been saying. Instead of asking God to heal me, I began thanking Him that He had healed me. I got it! I believed I was healed right then in that classroom!

Yet, it was a battle, because I didn't receive the results immediately. That's why 1 Timothy 6:12 says, "Fight the good fight of faith." I clung to the Scriptures that speak of healing and to my confession of healing. With perseverance I received the manifestation of my healing. Modern medicine did not have a cure for chronic fatigue syndrome, but God did. I thank God for doctors, and it's great when they can help, but their knowledge and ability are limited. God knows all things and can fix everything. He is the One who created us!

Healthy Aging

A lot of people struggle with aging. A friend of mine said she was tired of hearing how other women her age were speaking about their bodies. One woman said, "When I turned forty, my body just started falling apart." But my friend, said, "I'm not going to speak about my body that way. That's not what the Word of God says. In Psalm 103:5, the Word of God says, 'Thy youth is renewed like the eagle's,' and I'm going to confess *that*."

So what was the result? Well, she still looks younger than her age, she is beautiful, and she doesn't have any health issues. I'm not saying that her body isn't getting older, because it is. All of our bodies are aging. In 2 Corinthians 4:16, the Bible says that the outer man is decaying while the inward man is being renewed day by day, but we can be careful how we speak about the process.

Years ago, a fellow Bible School student noticed that he was getting a bald spot on his head, after his brother had already gone bald. At family gatherings, he was told he would go bald like his brother, it ran in their family. Determined to resist this, he found Proverbs 16:31 which says gray hair is a sign of wisdom, and he said to God, "Lord, if I keep going at this rate, I won't have any hair to turn gray." The Word of God was his foundation for faith. He began speaking over his hair, confessing that he would have gray hair as a sign of wisdom. As a result, that bald spot grew in. His family was amazed at what God had done for him. With God all things are possible!

**"Confession builds the road
over which faith
hauls its mighty cargo."** [4]
E. W. Kenyon

Chapter 9

The Word of God Brings Faith

**So then faith cometh by hearing,
and hearing by the word of God.
—Romans 10:17**

How do we develop our faith for healing or for anything else we need to receive from God?

Romans 12:3 says, "God hath dealt to every man the measure of faith." This tells us that, whether or not we feel like it, as born-again Christians, we all start out with the same measure of faith.

But if we haven't used our faith much, it may need to grow in order for us to be able to confidently speak faith-filled words.

How does our faith grow?—Does it grow by trying real hard to believe? No, it doesn't! Does it grow by prayer? No, it doesn't!

Romans 10:17 tells us that the **Word of God** increases our faith.

For example when Peter saw Jesus walking on the water, he said to Him "Lord, if it is You, command me to come to You on the water." (Matthew 14:27-30) NASB. Peter was saying to Jesus, "Command me." In essence he was saying, "Give me your Word."

Why?

Because faith is based on God's Word!

When Jesus said, "Come," Peter knew he would be able to do it. So based on his faith in the Lord's Word, Peter got out of the boat and walked on the water. Jesus would not have told him to come if he had not been able to do so. Therefore that Word gave Peter both the permission and the faith to walk on water.

Yet, Peter's walk on the water didn't last, did it? Seeing the wind, he became afraid and began to sink. As soon as he took his eyes off Jesus and the Word he had been given and instead focused on the wind and the waves, Peter began to sink! The circumstances brought fear, while the Word of God brought faith. We are supposed to walk by faith in God and not by what we see.

The Centurion's "Great Faith"

The Word of God also brought faith to the centurion, a Roman commander, whose servant had fallen ill.

Matthew 8:5-10, 13
And when Jesus was entered into Capernaum,
there came unto him a centurion, beseeching him,
And saying, Lord, my servant lieth at home sick of the
palsy, grievously tormented.
And Jesus saith unto him, I will come and heal him.
The centurion answered and said, Lord, I am not
worthy that thou shouldest come under my roof: but
speak the word only, and my servant shall be healed.
For I am a man under authority, having soldiers under
me: and I say to this man, Go, and he goeth;
and to another, Come, and he cometh; and to my
servant, Do this, and he doeth it.
When Jesus heard it, he marvelled, and said to
them that followed, Verily I say unto you, I have not
found so great faith, no, not in Israel...
And Jesus said unto the centurion, Go thy way;
and as thou hast believed, so be it done unto thee.
And his servant was healed in the selfsame hour.

The centurion said, "**Speak the word only**, and my
servant shall be healed." What was his faith based on?—
The Lord's Word! The centurion knew that if he could
get Jesus to call the servant healed, the servant would
be healed. He was ready to take Jesus at His **Word**. Jesus
called this "**great faith**."

What, then, is "great faith?"—Believing the Word
of God!

The same confidence that Peter and the centurion
placed in the spoken Word of Jesus, we can put into
the written Word of God, the Bible. The Bible is God
speaking to us today. Therefore the promises in His
Word are also for us. However, they are not necessarily
automatic. Instead, they are activated by believing them,

speaking them, and acting on them. God's Word gives us faith—faith to do what may seem impossible, because with God all things are possible!

What does the Word of God say about *your* situation? What Bible promises can *you* stand on? Those promises will give you the faith you need to speak the right words over your situation!

We need to keep our eyes on the Word of God, more than on our circumstances!

Meditating on God's Word Builds Faith

God gave Joshua directions after Moses' death. Joshua was not only new to leading Israel, but he was also facing the challenging task of taking the Israelites into the Promised Land. In this faith requiring situation, what did God tell Joshua to do to prepare himself for success?

Joshua 1:8
This book of the law shall not depart out of thy mouth; but thou shalt meditate therein day and night, that thou mayest observe to do according to all that is written therein: for then thou shalt make thy way prosperous, and then thou shalt have good success.

God told him that His Word should not "depart out of thy mouth." In other words, God said for Joshua to **confess the Word of God out loud—continually!**

The Hebrew word for "meditate," הגה, pronounced *hagah*," means "to mutter, to utter, to speak, to muse, to

68

declare, and to ponder." Not only are we to think on the Word, but we are also supposed to mutter it—to speak it to ourselves.

Focusing on and speaking the Word of God causes us to prosper and to be successful.

Chapter 10

"What did I rest from on the seventh day?"
—God

Confession is Work

Hebrews 11:3 NASB
By faith we understand that the worlds were prepared by the word of God, so that what is seen was not made out of things which are visible.

A few years ago, I was being extremely diligent with confession. I had many statements written down, and I was saying them several times a day. Adding that to my daily Bible reading and prayer became very time-consuming. The more I focused on confession, the more confessions I came up with. My list became longer and longer.

At one point I began to talk to God about it. I said, "Father, this is taking a lot of time." Out of my spirit I heard these words, "What did I rest from on the seventh day?" I answered, "You rested from Your work." "Yes," He said, "What was My work?" I thought about it for a moment then responded, "Your work was creating. You created the world." Then He said to me, "How did I create it?"

Suddenly I had the revelation. I said, "**Oh, with Words!**" Calling things into being is work!

Creating is work! Speaking the opposite of what you perceive with your senses is work! I understood what He was trying to get across to me!

God saw darkness and said, "Let there be light." For six days He spoke Words, creating and calling things into being. On the seventh day He rested from His work.— He rested from speaking Words, and He commanded us to rest on the seventh day, just as He had done.

In Genesis 2:3 NASB, it says, "Then God blessed the seventh day and sanctified it, because in it He rested from all His work which God had created and made."

What does that mean for the other six days of the week?—**It means we should be putting our words to work.**

Confession is work! Calling things into being, taming the tongue, and speaking out Scriptures from a place of faith are all work. It is easy to say what you see and feel; anyone can do that, but it takes discipline and time to train yourself to speak faith-filled words based on the Word of God.

Reinhard Bonnke the legendary African evangelist, said that God told him, " My Word in your mouth is just as powerful as My Word in My mouth." [5]

God has given us incredible creative power with **words**. We have the opportunity to create the future we desire with our faith-filled words!

The New Testament epistles are loaded with verses that tell us who we are in Christ and what we have in Him. We can confess Scriptures like Romans 8:37, "We are more than conquerors through him that loved us," and Phil. 4:13, "I can do all things through Christ which strengtheneth me."

Find Scriptures that apply to your situation. As you confess God's promises, they will become a reality in your life. The promises in God's Word are true, but they must be activated by believing and by speaking them.

To help you get started, there are key Scriptures in the Appendix of this book.

Appendix

**Charles Capps said God told him,
"I told My people they could have what they say,
but they are saying what they have." [6]**

As Christians, we are **followers of Jesus**. The Bible says in Ephesians 5:1, "Be ye therefore followers of God, as dear children." The word "followers" in Greek means "**imitators**." We are to imitate God, just as a child does his father. We are supposed to act like God and talk like Him.

When we study the life of Jesus, we see that He was tempted in all things, and yet He overcame. Since He was tempted in all things, He must also have been tempted in speech. And yet, He never spoke words of doubt or unbelief. He never spoke words of despair or failure. Instead, He spoke accurately, saying the same thing His Father was saying. He spoke the desired result and used the Word to defeat satan. He spoke about who He was, about His mission, and about His purpose here on earth.

We are to imitate Jesus, so—just as He was confessing who He was and what He was called to do—we should do the same.

Jesus is our model for words!

Jesus Confessed "I am"

The following Scriptures show Jesus confessing who He is:

- "I am the resurrection, and the life" (John 11:25).

- "I am the true vine" (John 15:1).

- "I am in the Father, and the Father in me" (John 14:11).

- "I am the Messiah" (John 4:25, 26, paraphrased).

- "I am the bread of life" (John 6:35).

- "I am the bread which came down out of heaven" (John 6:41).

- "I am the living bread" (John 6:51).

- "I know him: for I am from him, and he hath sent me" (John 7:29).

- "I am the light of the world" (John 8:12).

- "I know where I came from and where I am going" (John 8:14 NASB).

- "I am one that bear witness of myself, and the Father that sent me beareth witness of me" (John 8:18).

- "I am from above… I am not of this world" (John 8:23).

- "I proceeded forth and came from God" (John 8:42).

- "Before Abraham was, I am" (John 8:58).

- "I am the door of the sheep" (John 10:7).

- "I am the good shepherd" (John 10:11).

- "I and my Father are one" (John 10:30).

- "I am the Son of God" (John 10:36 NASB).

- "He that hath seen me hath seen the Father" (John 14:9).

Jesus Confessed His Mission

The following Scripture excerpts speak of His mission:

- "For I have come down from heaven, not to do My own will, but the will of Him who sent Me" (John 6:38 NASB).

- "I have come *as* Light into the world, so that everyone who believes in Me will not remain in darkness" (John 12:46 NASB).

- "I am the living bread that came down out of heaven; if anyone eats of this bread, he will live forever; and the bread also which I will give for the life of the world is My flesh" (John 6:51 NASB).

- "My teaching is not Mine, but His who sent Me" (John 7:16 NASB).

- "When you lift up the Son of Man, then you will know that I am *He*, and I do nothing on My own initiative, but I speak these things as the Father taught Me.

- "And He who sent Me is with Me; He has not left me alone, for I always do the things that are pleasing to Him" (John 8:28-29 NASB).

- "He sent me" (John 8:42).

- "I tell you the truth" (John 8:45).

- "I honour my Father" (John 8:49).

- "I must work the works of Him that sent Me" (John 9:4).

- "I am the door: by me if any man enter in, he shall be saved" (John 10:9).

- "I am come that they might have life, and that they might have it more abundantly" (John 10:10).

- "I am the good shepherd: the good shepherd giveth his life for the sheep" (John 10:11).

- "I showed you many good works from the Father" (John 10:32 NASB).

- "I am the Son of God … If I do not do the works of My Father, believe Me not. But if I do, though ye believe not me, believe the works: that ye may know, and believe, that the Father is in me, and I in him" (John 10:36-38).

- "Now is my soul troubled; and what shall I say? Father, save me from this hour: but for this cause came I unto this hour" (John 12:27-28).

- "I came forth from the Father, and am come into the world: again, I leave the world, and go to the Father" (John 16:28).

Confessions of The Believer's Identity:

So let's model after Him and confess (read out loud) what the Word of God says about us (paraphrased)!

- I am loved. I am a child of God. I am in God's family (1 John 3:1, 2).

- I am an heir of God. I am a joint heir with Christ. I confess my relationship with God. I have taken my place as His child (Romans 8:14, 16–17).

- In Him I live, and move, and have my being! I have life. I have energy and strength to move and to accomplish His will in my life (Acts 17:28).

- I abide in Him. I live in Him and His Word lives in me (John 15:5,7).

- I am a new creation. All things are new (2 Corinthians 5:17).

- I am His workmanship created in Christ Jesus for good works (Ephesians 2:10).

- I am righteous in Christ (2 Corinthians 5:21).

- I am in Christ. Now I am not condemned (Romans 8:1).

- I am wise in Christ. He is my wisdom. He is my righteousness, my sanctification, and my redemption (1 Corinthians 1:30).

- I have received abundance of grace and the gift of righteousness. I reign as a king in my life through

Jesus Christ (Romans 5:17).

- The love of God has been shed abroad in my heart. I have love to give — the God-kind-of-love (Romans 5:5).

- Love is patient, love is kind, and therefore I am patient, I am kind, and I do not seek my own; I am not easily provoked. I don't take into account a wrong suffered, because I have God's love in me (1 Corinthians 13:4).

- I have redemption. I have been redeemed from poverty, sickness, and spiritual death (Ephesians 1:7, Galatians 3:13, Deuteronomy 28).

- I am healed by the stripes that Jesus has taken (1 Peter 2:24).

- He Himself took my infirmities and carried away my diseases, and therefore I am healed (Matthew 8:17).

- Life in Christ Jesus set me free from sin and death (Romans 8:2).

- I have overcome, because greater is He that is in me (1 John 4:4).

- I am more than a conqueror through Him that loves me (Romans 8:37).

- Christ lives in me (Galatians 2:20).

- I am raised up to sit together with Him in heavenly places (Ephesians 2:6).

- My God supplies all my needs... I am well supplied. My God supplies all my needs according to His riches in glory by Christ Jesus (Philippians 4:19).

- I have been blessed with all spiritual blessings in the heavenly places in Christ (Ephesians 1:3).

Confessions of The Believer's Mission:

Like Jesus, let's confess what our mission is!

- I love God, and I love my neighbor (Mark 12:33, Galatians 5:14).

- I am a minister of reconciliation. I lead people to Jesus (2 Corinthians 5:17–21).

- I am God's workmanship created in Christ for good works (Ephesians 2:10).

- He chose me and appointed me, that I should go and bear fruit, and that my fruit should remain (John 15:16).

- I make disciples of all nations, baptizing them in the Name of the Father, the Son and the Holy Spirit (Matthew 28:18–19).

- I go into the world and preach the gospel to all creation, and these signs accompany me, because I am a believer. I lay hands on the sick, and they recover (Mark 16:15–18).

- A new commandment He gave to me that I love others, even as He loves me. By this all men know that I am His disciple because I love others (John 13:34–35).

- I abide in Him and His words abide in me so I can ask whatever I wish and it shall be done for me (John 15:7).

- I love my enemies, and pray for those who persecute

me (Matthew 5:44).

- I am a doer of the word not a hearer only
  (James 1:22).

- I live by faith (Habakkuk 2:4).

- I am not conformed to this world but I am
  transformed by the renewing of my mind on the
  word of God (Romans 12:2).

- The Bible does not depart form my mouth but I
  meditate on it day and night, so that I am careful
  to do all that is written in it; therefore my way is
  prosperous and I have success (Joshua 1:8).

- I rejoice always; pray without ceasing; in everything
  I give thanks for this is God's will for me in Christ
  Jesus (1 Thessalonians 5:16–18).

- I take every thought captive to the obedience of
  Christ (2 Corinthians 10:5).

- I am anxious for nothing, but in everything by
  prayer and supplication with thanksgiving I let my
  requests be made known to God. And the peace of
  God, which surpasses all comprehension, guards my
  heart and mind in Christ Jesus. Whatever is true,
  honorable, right, pure, lovely, of good repute, I let me
  mind dwell on these things (Philippians 4:6–8).

- I let no unwholesome word proceed from my mouth,
  only words that edify and give grace to the hearers
  (Ephesians 4:29).

- I am kind, tender-hearted, forgiving, just as God in
  Christ has forgiven me (Ephesians 4:32).

- I go and preach saying, "the kingdom of heaven is at

hand, heal the sick, raise the dead, cleanse the lepers, cast out demons, freely I received, freely I give" (Matthew 10:8).

- Forgetting what lies behind and reaching forward to what lies ahead, I press on toward the goal for the prize of the upward call of God in Christ Jesus (Philippians 3:13–14).

- I can do all things through Christ who strengthens me (Philippians 4:13).

My Personal Confessions:

_____

_____

_____

_____

_____

_____

_____

_____

_____

_____

_____

_____

_____

_____

_____

_____

My Personal Confessions:

_____

_____

_____

_____

_____

_____

_____

_____

_____

_____

_____

_____

_____

_____

_____

_____

My Personal Confessions:

My Personal Confessions:

My Personal Confessions:

My Personal Confessions:

End Notes

1. Kenneth E. Hagin, Biblical Keys to Financial Prosperity (Tulsa, Oklahoma: Faith Library Publications, 1995), pp. 71-73.

2. Mark Hankins, Never Run at Your Giant With Your Mouth Shut (Alexandra, La: MHM Publications, 2001), p. 6.

3. F.F. Bosworth, Christ the Healer (Grand Rapids, Michigan: Fleming H. Revel/Baker Book House Company, 1973), p. 143.

4. Don Gossett & E. W. Kenyon, The Power of Your Words (Blane, Washington, Don and Joyce Gossett, 1977), p. 32.

5. Ron Steele, Plundering Hell to Populate Heaven: The Reinhard Bonnke Story (Tulsa, Oklahoma: Albury Press, 1987), p. 47.

6. Charles Capps, The Tongue – A Creative Force (Tulsa, Oklahoma: Harrison House, Inc.1995), p. 163.

A Prayer to Receive Jesus as Savior

Dear God,

I come to you in the Name of Jesus.

Your Word says, "...the one who comes to me I will certainly not cast out" (John 6:27). Therefore I know you won't cast me out, but you receive me and I thank you.

You said in Your Word, "...WHOEVER WILL CALL UPON THE NAME OF THE LORD WILL BE SAVED" (Rom. 10:13).

You also said,"...if you confess with your mouth Jesus as Lord, and believe in your heart that God raised Him from the dead, you shall be saved; for with the heart man believes, resulting in righteousness, and with the mouth he confesses, resulting in salvation" (Rom. 10:9-10).

I am calling upon the Name of the Lord Jesus Christ right now. I do believe in my heart, and I confess Jesus as my Lord.

Thank you for giving me salvation and becoming my Father.

Signed _____

Date _____

About the Author

GiGi Allen is a gifted, insightful teacher who travels within the U.S. and also overseas ministering the Word of God. GiGi and her husband Brad founded and pastor Victory International Church in San Mateo, California. A full time minister ordained through RHEMA Bible Training Center, she served for many years as an Instructor and the Dean of Victory Bible School. GiGi is also a graduate of both San Jose State University and of RHEMA.

For scheduling meetings or purchasing
additional material, please contact:

GiGi Allen
P.O. Box 5425
San Mateo, CA 94402
Phone (650) 655-4748
Internet www.VictoryIC.org

Materials by GiGi Allen

Books
1. The Creative Power of Your Words
2. Bible Highlights
3. Walking with God (workbook)
4. Growing in God's Love (workbook)
5. Forgiving (mini book)
6. Scriptures in Color Volume 1-5 (coloring books)
7. Scriptures in Color in Spanish

CD's
1. To Build You Up
2. Powerful, Effective Prayer (3 CD set)
3. How to be Led by the Spirit of God (4 CD set)
4. Faith Foundation (4 CD set)
5. Redemptive Realities (4 CD set)
6. Giving to the Lord (2 CD set)
7. The life of Christ (4 CD set)
8. Scriptural Faith
9. How Faith Comes
10. Faith Requires Action
11. Faith & Healing
12. Mastering Your Thoughts
13. What Did God Rest From?
14. Words
15. Healing is God's Will

Made in the USA
Middletown, DE
03 March 2020